DINOSAURS

CARNIVORES

by Dougal Dixon

Gareth Stevens Publishing
A WORLD ALMANAC EDUCATION GROUP COMPANY

CONTENTS

Please visit our web site at:
www.garethstevens.com
For a free color catalog describing Gareth
Stevens' list of high-quality books and
multimedia programs, call 1-800-542-2595
(USA) or 1-800-461-9120 (Canada). Gareth
Stevens Publishing's Fax: (414) 332-3567.

Library of Congress Cataloging-in-Publication Data
available upon request from publisher. Fax (414) 336-0157
for the attention of the Publishing Records Department.

ISBN 0-8368-2915-8

This edition first published in 2001 by
Gareth Stevens Publishing
A World Almanac Education Group Company
330 West Olive Street, Suite 100
Milwaukee, WI 53212 USA

This U.S. edition © 2001 by Gareth Stevens, Inc.
First published by ticktock Publishing Ltd., Century
Place, Lamberts Road, Tunbridge Wells, Kent TN2
3EH, U.K. Original edition © 2001 ticktock
Publishing Ltd. Additional end matter © 2001 by
Gareth Stevens, Inc.

Illustrations: John Alston, Lisa Alderson,
Dougal Dixon, Simon Mendez, Luis Rey
Gareth Stevens editor: David K. Wright
Cover design: Katherine Kroll
Consultant: Paul Mayer, Geology Collections
Manager, Milwaukee Public Museum

Printed in Hong Kong

1 2 3 4 5 6 7 8 9 05 04 03 02 01

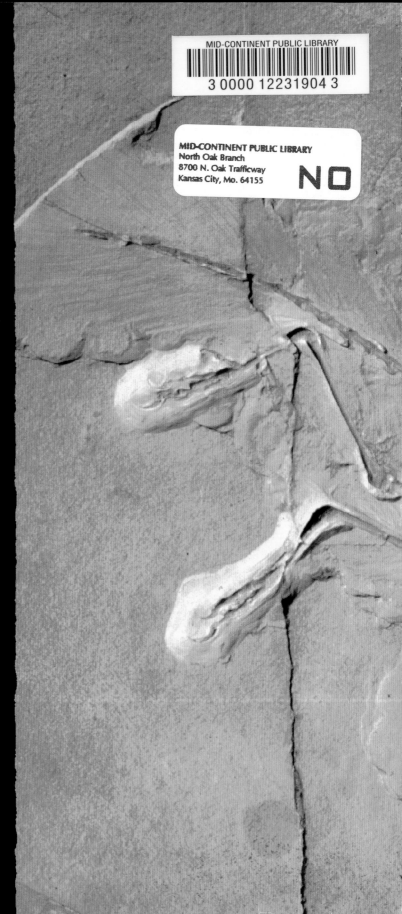

CARNIVORES

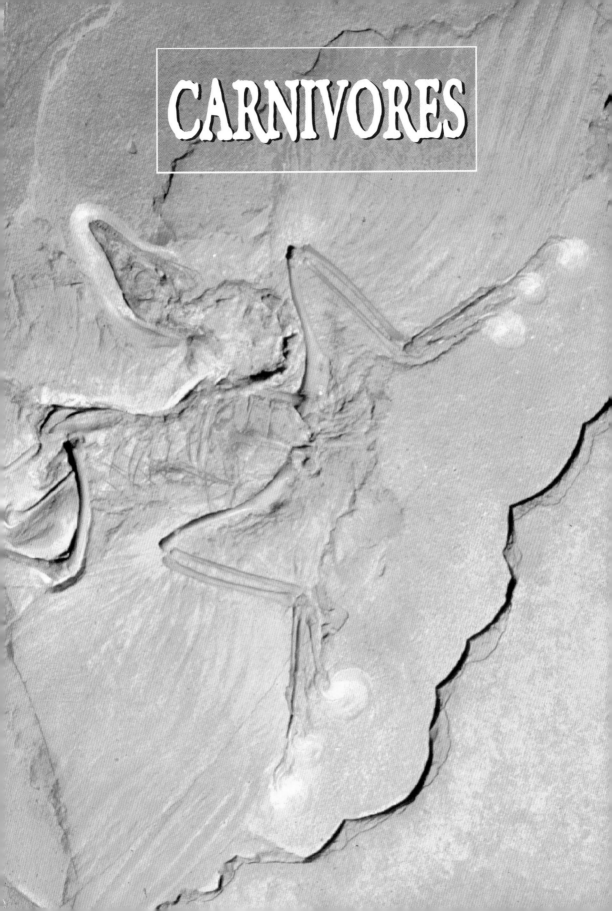

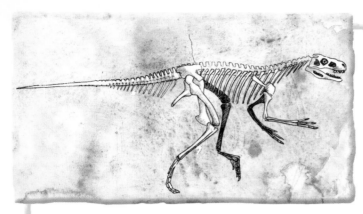

POWERFUL LEGS

Herrerasaurus, a meat-eating dinosaur, walked on strong hind legs with its teeth and the claws on its arms held out in front, where they could do the most damage. *Herrerasaurus*'s back was held horizontally, and the body was balanced by a long tail. This structure became the pattern for all meat-eating dinosaurs.

BEFORE THE DINOSAURS

During the Permian Period, the main plant-eating animals of the time were mammal-like reptiles. They had teeth like mammals, and some were even hairy. The biggest, such as the broad-headed *Moschops*, shown here, were built like hippopotami. At about the same time as the first dinosaurs evolved, the first mammals evolved, too. Descended from the mammal-like reptiles, they were small and furry and bore live young. If the dinosaurs had not come to prominence, the mammals might have taken over. Instead, they had to wait 160 million years before evolving into more successful species.

EORAPTOR

Eoraptor was about the size of a fox and, like all the dinosaurs to follow, walked on legs that were held straight under its body. This structure made it a much faster animal than the other reptiles that walked on legs sprawled out to the side.

TIGER-SIZED

Herrerasaurus was about the size of a tiger and thus was a much bigger animal than *Eoraptor*. One of the first dinosaurs, it was a primitive theropod, part of the group that includes all the meat eaters. Adults could reach a length of 10 feet (3 m). The skeleton of a *Herrerasaurus* was found in Argentina, in South America.

WHERE DID THEY COME FROM?

Dinosaurs! The most famous of all extinct animals, these reptiles, most of them whale-sized, dominated Earth for about 160 million years. Reptiles evolved during the Carboniferous Period, about 350 million years ago, and flourished in the succeeding Permian, Triassic, Jurassic, and Cretaceous periods. During this time, there were land-living reptiles, swimming reptiles, flying reptiles, herbivores (plant eaters), carnivores (meat eaters), and omnivores (both plant and meat eaters) — reptiles of all kinds in every environment. The age of reptiles was well under way before the first dinosaurs appeared around the end of the Triassic Period, about 225 million years ago. At the end of the Cretaceous Period, about 65 million years ago, all the big reptiles died out, and mammals took over.

EORAPTOR SKULL

An x-ray photograph of *Eoraptor's* skull shows how its lightweight skull was made up of thin struts of bone. The dinosaur's light bone structure enabled it to move fast. The skulls of most subsequent meat-eating dinosaurs were built like this.

RAUISUCHIAN

Before the dinosaurs came along, the biggest of the hunters was a group of land-living crocodile relatives called rauisuchians. They had big heads and many sharp teeth, and, although they were slow-moving, they were faster than the plant-eating reptiles that abounded at the time.

CARBONIFEROUS 354-290 MYA	PERMIAN 290-248 MYA	TRIASSIC 248-206 MYA	EARLY/MID JURASSIC 206-159 MYA	LATE JURASSIC 159-144 MYA

LIKE MEGALOSAURUS?

For a long time, the name *Megalosaurus* was applied to the fossil of any meat-eating dinosaur found in Britain or Europe. All kinds of unrelated dinosaurs were erroneously given the name. Only now is this mixture of different animals being sorted out. One of the dinosaurs once thought to be a *Megalosaurus* is a virtually complete skeleton of *Eustreptospondylus* in the Oxford University Museum in England.

MEGALOSAURUS JAW

The lower jawbone and teeth of *Megalosaurus* were the first parts of the animal to be discovered. They were found in Oxfordshire, England, in about 1815. The Reverend William Buckland studied them and deduced from the sharp, pointed teeth that they had belonged to a meat-eating animal and that it had been a large reptile. Other scientists studied the remains in the 1820s and one of them — history does not tell us who — came up with the name *Megalosaurus*.

FIRST DINOSAUR THEME PARK

Because of the great public interest in science in the mid-19th century, part of Crystal Palace park in South London was developed as an ancient landscape. Statues (which still stand today) were erected showing the three dinosaurs and the marine reptiles that were known at the time. All that was known of *Megalosaurus* was its jawbone, teeth, and a few fragments of bone. Since nobody knew what the animal actually looked like, it was modeled as a fearsome, four-footed, dragonlike creature.

TRIASSIC 248-206 MYA	EARLY/MID JURASSIC 206-159 MYA	LATE JURASSIC 159-144 MYA	EARLY CRETACEOUS 144-97 MYA	LATE CRETACEOUS 97-65 MYA

THE FIRST KNOWN

Since civilization began, people have known about giant bones embedded in rocks. In earliest times they were spoken of in legends as the bones of giants and dragons and other mythical creatures. By the early 19th century, however, scientific knowledge had advanced sufficiently for scientists to appreciate the true nature of fossils. In 1842, the British anatomist, Sir Richard Owen, invented the term "dinosauria" (terrible lizards) to classify three fossil animals whose skeletons had been discovered in England during the previous two decades. One was the plant-eating *Iguanodon*, which is now quite well known. Another was the armored *Hylaeosaurus*, which we still know very little about. The first of the trio to be brought to light and described was the carnivorous *Megalosaurus*.

WILLIAM BUCKLAND (1784–1856)

This 19th-century clergyman was typical of his time. When not in the pulpit, he spent his extensive spare time doing scientific research. Most of the fossils he studied were of sea-living animals — seashells and marine reptiles. Fossils of land-living animals have always been more rare (*see page 34*). He may not have invented the name *Megalosaurus*, but he was the scholar who did all the scientific work on it.

MODERN VIEW

Even today, we do not have a clear idea of what *Megalosaurus* looked like because so few fossilized remains have been found. Like all meat-eating dinosaurs, it must have walked on its hind legs with its big head held well forward, balanced by a heavy tail. Fossils found in lagoon deposits in what is now Normandy in northern France suggest that *Megalosaurus* was a shoreline scavenger that prowled the beach, eating dead things that had been washed up.

EARLY HUNTERS

Most early meat-eating dinosaurs were small, some no bigger than our cats and dogs. They probably fed mainly on even smaller animals, such as lizards and early mammals. However, most plant-eating reptiles of the time were large animals and would also have made good prey for meat eaters. Some of the early dinosaurs adopted a strategy of hunting in packs so they could bring down and kill some of these big plant eaters. Today, such teamwork is still used in the wild by animals such as Canadian wolves, which hunt moose bigger than themselves. Similarly, on the African plains, groups of hyenas attack wildebeest that are far bigger than they are.

THE CONNECTICUT FOOTPRINTS

At the beginning of the 19th century, long before anybody knew anything about dinosaurs, farmers in New England kept finding three-toed trackways in Triassic sandstone at the foot of the Appalachian Mountains, shown above. At first it was believed the footprints were made by giant birds that existed in the area before Noah's flood, as described in the Bible. We now know they were footprints of dinosaur packs, probably made by *Coelophysis* or something that resembled *Coelophysis*.

TRIASSIC 248-206 MYA	EARLY/MID JURASSIC 206-159 MYA	LATE JURASSIC 159-144 MYA	EARLY CRETACEOUS 144-97 MYA	LATE CRETACEOUS 97-65 MYA

BIRD & DINOSAUR FOOTPRINTS

Birds and dinosaurs are so closely related it is little wonder the footprints of one could be mistaken for those of the other. In a series of ridges of Jurassic and Cretaceous rocks in the flanks of the Rocky Mountains west of Denver, there are fossilized footprints of both dinosaurs and birds. Bird footprints can be distinguished from dinosaur prints by the greater spread of their toes — about 90° as opposed to about 45°. There is also often a trace of the little fourth toe pointing backward. In dinosaurs, this toe is usually well clear of the ground.

DINOSAUR

BIRD

ONE WORLD

In Late Triassic and Early Jurassic times, Earth was very different from the way it is today. All the continental landmasses were joined together in one area, called Pangaea. Since there was only one landmass, animals of the same kind were able to migrate everywhere. This is why we find the remains of almost identical animals in New Mexico and in Connecticut, as well as in Zimbabwe, thousands of miles away on the African continent.

SYNTARSUS

In 1972, a remarkable deposit of fossils was found in Rhodesia (now Zimbabwe). A mass of bones lay in fine river sediment, sandwiched between rocks formed from sand dunes. The fossils were of a pack of small, meat-eating dinosaurs of different sizes and ages. They seemed to have drowned in a flash flood that struck as they were crossing a dry river bed. These meat-eating dinosaurs, named *Syntarsus*, were almost identical in build to *Coelophysis*, and some scientists believe they were a species of the same animal.

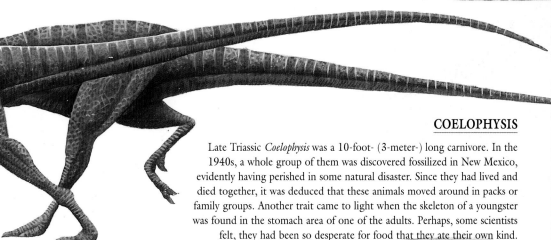

COELOPHYSIS

Late Triassic *Coelophysis* was a 10-foot- (3-meter-) long carnivore. In the 1940s, a whole group of them was discovered fossilized in New Mexico, evidently having perished in some natural disaster. Since they had lived and died together, it was deduced that these animals moved around in packs or family groups. Another trait came to light when the skeleton of a youngster was found in the stomach area of one of the adults. Perhaps, some scientists felt, they had been so desperate for food that they ate their own kind.

CREST-HEADED BEASTS

Look at the bright colors of many birds — the long tail feathers of a peacock, the gaudy bill of a toucan, the red breast of a robin. Color is part of a bird's method of communication. A bird's brain can "read" the colors it sees, enabling the bird to recognize whether another bird is a friend or foe. Birds are related to dinosaurs (*see pages 22–23*), which had similar brains and senses. It is very likely that dinosaurs also used color for communication. Some dinosaurs (especially among the carnivores) had crests and horns as brightly colored as the plumage of modern birds.

DILOPHOSAURUS IN LIFE

When it was alive, *Dilophosaurus* probably looked dazzling. Its crests may have been particularly colorful to frighten rivals or attract a mate from far away. The rest of the animal, including its dewlaps (flaps of skin beneath the chin), may also have been brightly colored to back up the signals given by the crests.

FORWARD THINKING

The Early Jurassic meat eater from Antarctica, *Cryolophosaurus*, had a crest that curled up and forward above its eyes. The bony core was probably covered with brightly colored horn or skin. *Cryolophosaurus* is the only dinosaur known to have had a crest that ran across the skull, from side to side, rather than along it, from front to back. At 26 feet (8 m) long, it was probably the biggest meat eater of its time, its size enhanced by the crest.

HORNED MONSTER

In the Late Jurassic, one of the fiercest dinosaurs, *Ceratosaurus*, lived in North America and Tanzania. It had a heavy head with a horn on the nose and two horns above the eyes. The heavy skull suggests they may have fought by head butting, but the horns were lightly built and would not have been much use as weapons.

MONOLOPHOSAURUS

The crest of *Monolophosaurus*, a medium-sized, Middle Jurassic, meat-eating dinosaur from China, was made up of a pair of skull bones fused together and growing upward. Air gaps and channels between the bones were connected to the nostrils and may have amplified grunts and roars generated in the animal's throat. In this way the crest would have helped it communicate.

DILOPHOSAURUS SKELETON

Dilophosaurus was a bear-sized, meat-eating dinosaur from Early Jurassic North America. The first skeleton found had semicircular plate-like structures lying near it. Later finds showed that these structures were crests that ran parallel to one another along the length of the skull. However, what no skeleton can ever tell us is what color the crests were in life.

TRIASSIC 248-206 MYA	EARLY/MID JURASSIC 206-159 MYA	LATE JURASSIC 159-144 MYA	EARLY CRETACEOUS 144-97 MYA	LATE CRETACEOUS 97-65 MYA

HEAVY CLAW

Baryonyx was discovered by an amateur fossil collector in southern England in 1983. The skeleton was so complete that it gave us the first clear view of what these animals looked like. *Baryonyx* was an unusual meat-eating dinosaur that had crocodile-like jaws packed with sharp teeth and long forelimbs with hooked claws, which were used to catch fish.

Baryonyx stood 10 feet (3 m) tall, and each of its claws measured nearly 1 foot (35 centimeters) long. We think that it ranged over a large area stretching from England to North Africa.

MENACING MIMIC

Suchomimus was found in a remote dune-covered area of the Sahara in 1998 by a team from the United States and Niger. A huge predatory dinosaur with a skull like a crocodile's and huge thumb claws, it measured 36 feet (11 m) long and 12 feet (4 m) high at the hip. The thumb claws and powerful forelimbs were used to snare prey, and the thin sail along its back, which reached a height of 2 feet (0.5 m) over the hips, may have been brightly colored for display.

SPINOSAURUS

SPINOSAURUS — 50 feet (15 m) long, 24 feet (7 m) high

SUCHOMIMUS — 36 feet (11 m) long, 12 feet (4 m) high

BARYONYX — 32 feet (10 m) long, 10 feet (3 m) high

IRRITATOR — 21 feet (6 m) long, 6 feet (2 m) high

BARYONYX

BIG BITE

Many modern reptiles have features that are similar to those of the spinosaurids. Crocodiles and alligators, for example, have long jaws and many teeth, and they hunt for fish in a similar way. Like the spinosaurids, they were for a long time wrongly suspected of eating their young.

SPINOSAURIDS - THE FISH EATERS

We normally think of fish-eating animals as creatures that live in the water. However, there are many land-living animals that like to eat fish, too. Grizzly bears are often seen beside waterfalls hooking out migrating salmon as they leap to their spawning grounds, and otters live mostly on land but hunt fish. It was the same in the Jurassic Period. One particular family of land-dwelling dinosaurs — the spinosaurids — seems to have been particularly well equipped for fishing. They had long jaws with many small teeth and a big claw on each hand. They lived in Early Cretaceous times, and their remains have been found across the world, from southern England to North Africa and South America.

SUCHOMIMUS

IRRITATOR

SPINY CUSTOMER

Spinosaurus was excavated in Egypt in 1915. Unfortunately, the remains were destroyed when its museum in Germany was bombed in World War II. What we do know about it was that it was as big as *Tyrannosaurus* and had a fin down its back almost 6.5 feet (2 m) tall. The fin was probably used to cool the animal in hot weather. In 1999, a U.S. expedition found its original quarry in Egypt, so there may be hope of finding new specimens.

AN IRRITATING EXAMPLE

Irritator was given its name because of the confusing circumstances in which it was found. The skull — all that we have of the animal — was collected in Brazil sometime in the 1990s and sent to the museum in Stuttgart, Germany. But then the museum staff had a surprise. Whoever dug it up and sold it to the museum had added pieces to it and stuck it together with car body filler to make it look much more spectacular. Now that we have had a good look at it, we can tell that it is a small spinosaurid.

TRIASSIC 248-206 MYA	EARLY/MID JURASSIC 206-159 MYA	LATE JURASSIC 159-144 MYA	EARLY CRETACEOUS 144-97 MYA	LATE CRETACEOUS 97-65 MYA

NQWEBASAURUS

Scientists became very excited in the late 1990s when they found the almost complete skeleton of a 3-foot- (1-m-) long *Nqwebasaurus* embedded in Lower Cretaceous rocks in South Africa. It proved that the family to which most of the small meat-eating dinosaurs belonged (the coelurosaurids) had existed in the southern continents during the Cretaceous period, as well as in North America, Europe, and Asia.

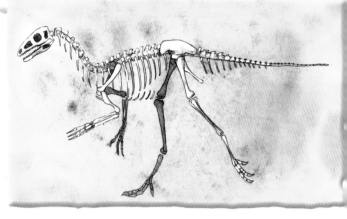

ITALIAN BEAUTY

In the 1990s, this beautifully preserved skeleton of *Scipionyx* was found in Lower Cretaceous rocks in Italy. It was so finely fossilized that even some of the soft anatomy (the lungs and intestines) were preserved. Their existence confirms that this animal, probably along with all other small dinosaurs, was able to breathe efficiently while running. This would have made it an energetic and active hunter. The way the bones were articulated indicates that this specimen of *Scipionyx*, only 10 inches (25 cm) long, was not yet fully grown.

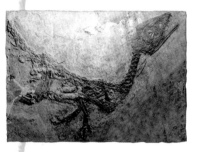

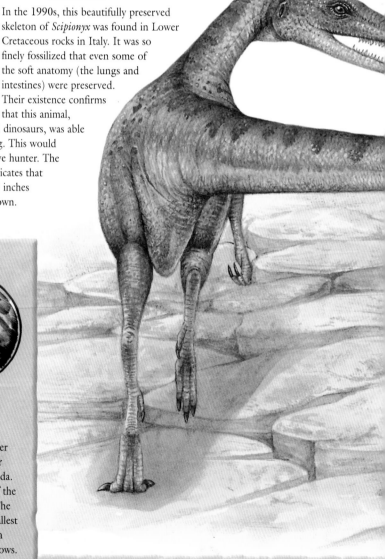

TINIEST FOOTPRINT

In the 1970s, the tiny footprint of a dinosaur that could have been no bigger than a thrush was found in the Upper Triassic rocks of Newfoundland in Canada. The arrangement of the toes is typical of the meat-eating dinosaurs of the Triassic. The print is the only trace we have of the smallest dinosaur ever found. Whether it was a youngster or fully grown, nobody yet knows.

THE SMALLEST DINOSAURS

When we think of *dinosaurs* (a name that comes from words meaning "monstrous lizards" or "terrifying lizards"), we usually visualize the huge, fierce animals that have captured our imagination. Some dinosaurs, however, were actually not much bigger than a chicken. Scuttling around among the giants, small dinosaurs were probably more common than big ones. Unfortunately, as their skeletons were so delicate, few have been preserved as fossils. And yet, some good specimens have been found, many preserved in detail.

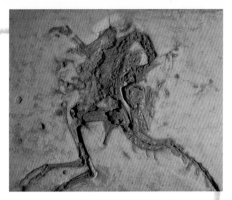

COMPSOGNATHUS SKELETON

Two *Compsognathus* skeletons have been found: one in France, the other in Germany. The German specimen, which was well preserved in limestone, displays the skeleton and contents of its stomach, showing that its last meal included a small lizard. Some scientists thought *Compsognathus* was the baby of some other dinosaur, but the blobs scattered around the skeleton are probably eggs, proving that this was an adult.

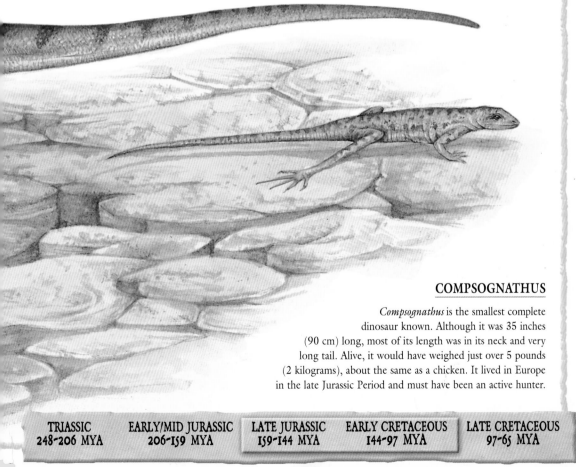

COMPSOGNATHUS

Compsognathus is the smallest complete dinosaur known. Although it was 35 inches (90 cm) long, most of its length was in its neck and very long tail. Alive, it would have weighed just over 5 pounds (2 kilograms), about the same as a chicken. It lived in Europe in the late Jurassic Period and must have been an active hunter.

TRIASSIC 248-206 MYA	EARLY/MID JURASSIC 206-159 MYA	LATE JURASSIC 159-144 MYA	EARLY CRETACEOUS 144-97 MYA	LATE CRETACEOUS 97-65 MYA

SKULL

A typical *Allosaurus* skull is about 3.5 feet (1 m) long. The jaws were armed with more than 70 teeth, some measuring 3 inches (8 cm). The teeth were curved, pointed, and serrated, ideal for ripping the flesh of large plant-eating dinosaurs. The joints between the skull bones would have allowed the snout to move up and down to help manipulate food. The lower jaws were hinged so they could expand sideways to allow the animal to gulp down big chunks of meat.

JURASSIC GIANT

Some dinosaurs really did live up to their reputation of being enormous, fearsome beasts. Probably the most terrifying animal of the Late Jurassic Period was *Allosaurus*. Its remains have been found in the rocks known as the Morrison Formation, which stretches down the western United States from the Canadian border to New Mexico. These deposits yielded the most important dinosaur discoveries made in the second half of the 19th century. Over a hundred different kinds of dinosaur (mostly plant eaters) were found there. The most powerful of the meat eaters found was *Allosaurus.*

MUSCLES

By studying the arrangement of bones in the skeleton and seeing the points of attachment for individual muscles, scientists have figured out what a living *Allosaurus* would have looked like. The leg muscles would have allowed it to move at speeds of up to 18 miles (30 km) per hour — not particularly swift but fast enough to catch the slow-moving herbivores of the time. The neck muscles would have been massive to control the huge head and powerful jaws.

FEET

The feet of *Allosaurus* had three powerful toes, muscular enough to carry the entire weight of the adult, which must have been over a ton. Unlike its fingers, the toes were not equipped with hooked claws but with broad hooves that would have helped bear the great weight. The legs were not particularly long for the size of animal and were evidently not built for speed.

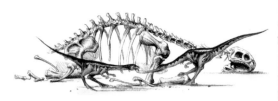

HUNTING

The bones of plant eaters such as *Camarasaurus* are found throughout the Morrison Formation, often mixed up with the broken teeth of meat-eating dinosaurs. Discoveries like these suggest that the big plant eaters — especially sick ones — were often attacked and killed by big meat eaters like *Allosaurus*. Once the killer had eaten its fill, packs of smaller meat eaters (*see pages 8-9*) may have scavenged what was left.

FOREARMS

Allosaurus's hands had three claws: one claw, at 10 inches (25 cm) long, was much larger than the other two. The joint on this first finger allowed the huge claw to turn inward. *Allosaurus* would have been able to grasp its prey, kill it, then rip it apart. The span of its hand would have been wide enough to grasp the head of an adult man, had there been such a person around in Jurassic times!

ALLOSAURUS IN LIFE

We have a fairly good idea what *Allosaurus* looked like from the thousands of bones (some almost complete skeletons) that have been found. These bones belonged to juveniles that measured about 10 feet (3 m) from nose to tail-tip and to adults of about 30 feet (9 m) long. Some of the bones found must have come from 40-foot (12-m) monsters. Mounted casts of *Allosaurus* skeletons can be seen in many museums around the world. The actual bones are too heavy to mount and are usually kept behind the scenes for research.

TRIASSIC 248-206 MYA	EARLY/MID JURASSIC 206-159 MYA	LATE JURASSIC 159-144 MYA	EARLY CRETACEOUS 144-97 MYA	LATE CRETACEOUS 97-65 MYA

FAST HUNTERS

Back in the late 1800s and early 1900s, scientists developed a theory that birds and dinosaurs were related. This theory fell out of favor for a long time but was revived in the 1960s when a group of dinosaurs, extremely birdlike in their build, was discovered. They ranged from the size of a goose to the size of a tiger and had winglike joints in their forearms. They also had strong hind legs with huge, sickle-like killing claws on their feet, showing that they were fast runners and fierce hunters. These dinosaurs are known as the dromaeosaurids (part of a larger group called maniraptorans) and are commonly referred to as "raptors."

BIRD OR DROMAEOSAURID?

Right down to the killing claw on its foot, *Rahonavis*, an Early Cretaceous bird from Madagascar, had the skeleton of a dromaeosaurid. If it had not been for the functional wings, it would have been grouped with the dromaeosaurids.

TERRIBLE CLAWS

The skeleton of a plant-eating *Tenontosaurus*, found in Lower Cretaceous rocks in Montana, was surrounded by the remains of several *Deinonychus*. *Deinonychus* probably hunted in packs, surrounded its prey, and slashed it to death. *Deinonychus* could have stood on one foot and slashed with the other, or it may have hung onto its prey with its clawed hands and slashed away with both hind feet, as cats do.

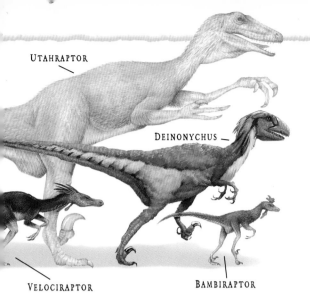

UTAHRAPTOR

DEINONYCHUS

VELOCIRAPTOR

BAMBIRAPTOR

A RANGE OF DROMAEOSAURIDS

About the size of a goose, *Bambiraptor* is the smallest dromaeosaurid. Turkey-sized *Velociraptor* is probably the best known. Scientists were first alerted to the birdlike nature of these animals in the 1960s, when tiger-sized *Deinonychus* was discovered. Bigger dromaeosaurids are only known from fragments of bone. *Utahraptor* probably weighed more than a ton, while *Megaraptor* (not shown), known only from a 13-inch (34-cm) killing claw, must have approached the size of the big meat eaters, such as *Allosaurus* (*see pages 16–17*). Most of these animals were found in Upper Cretaceous rocks in North America.

EARLY BIRD

This fossil of the first bird *Archaeopteryx*, dating from the Late Jurassic, was found in Germany in 1877. If it had not been for the fossil's feather impressions, the skeleton would have been mistaken for that of a dinosaur because it has a toothed jaw, clawed hands, and a long tail. As well as evolving into modern birds, some of *Archaeopteryx*'s descendants may have lost their powers of flight and developed into meat-eating dromaeosaurids.

BAMBIRAPTOR

Any doubts about whether dromaeosaurids were related to birds were finally put to rest in the late 1990s, when an almost complete skeleton of *Bambiraptor* was discovered in Upper Cretaceous rocks in Montana. Every bone seems to be a bird bone, every joint a bird joint. It was no doubt a warm-blooded animal that was covered with feathers.

TRIASSIC 248-206 MYA	EARLY/MID JURASSIC 206-159 MYA	LATE JURASSIC 159-144 MYA	EARLY CRETACEOUS 144-97 MYA	LATE CRETACEOUS 97-65 MYA

TROODON

Troodon was one of the maniraptorans, although it was not quite as birdlike as the dromaeosaurids. This small meat eater of the late Cretaceous Period was about 8 feet (2.5 m) long and may well have had feathers.

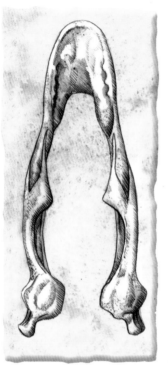

CAENAGNATHUS JAWBONE

Caenagnathus was a dinosaur that probably resembled *Oviraptor* and may have been an egg eater. Certainly, its toothless lower jaw was quite wide in the middle and would have been good for swallowing eggs. As no other remains have been found, *Caenagnathus* remains a bit of a mystery.

OVIRAPTOR HEAD

An *Oviraptor's* head makes it easy to believe it might be an egg eater. Its very short, beaklike mouth and its gullet, situated over the widest part of its jaw, were ideal for swallowing something big and round. As in modern egg-eating snakes, two bones protruding down from its palate were perfectly positioned to tear open an egg on its way down. With its long fingers, which were just right for grasping eggs, *Oviraptor* may have been an egg-eating dinosaur after all. There seems to have been little else for it to eat on the desert plains of Late Cretaceous Mongolia.

EGG THIEF

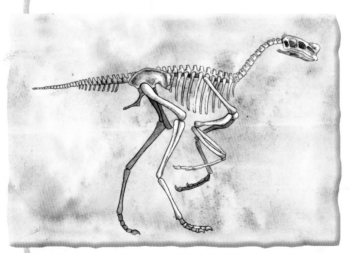

The jaw of *Caenagnathus* was similar to that of *Chirostenotes*, a turkey-sized dinosaur with very long fingers that would have enabled it to pick up mollusks and insects or raid other dinosaur nests for their eggs. Perhaps there were many different kinds of egg-stealing dinosaurs in Late Cretaceous times.

TRIASSIC 248-206 MYA	EARLY/MID JURASSIC 206-159 MYA	LATE JURASSIC 159-144 MYA	EARLY CRETACEOUS 144-97 MYA	LATE CRETACEOUS 97-65 MYA

EGGS & NESTS

Like modern birds, some dinosaurs built nests and laid eggs. The first known dinosaur nests were found by an expedition sent to the Gobi Desert from the American Museum of Natural History in 1923. The nests were among remains of herds of the horned dinosaur *Protoceratops*. Alongside the supposed *Protoceratops* eggs lay the skeleton of a toothless meat eater, *Oviraptor*. This so-called "egg thief" was thought to have been buried in a sandstorm while digging up the eggs. As sometimes happens, however, more evidence caused later paleontologists to re-evaluate this interpretation. In the 1990s, another expedition to the Gobi Desert found the fossil of an *Oviraptor* sitting on a nest, incubating eggs, which meant those first nests must also have been *Oviraptor* nests!

TROODON EGGS

Fossils of *Troodon* nests show they were oval ridges of mud surrounding the eggs, very much like the nests of *Oviraptor*. The eggs were laid in pairs, which suggests that the dinosaur had a pair of oviducts (egg tubes) within its body. A modern bird has only one oviduct. Birds have evolved many such features, which keep down their body weight to make flying easier.

NESTING DINOSAUR

In the 1990s, a fossil of an *Oviraptor* was found sitting on a nest with its arms spread protectively around some eggs, evidently keeping them warm with its body heat. Modern birds do this, since their feathers provide insulation. This is one piece of evidence suggesting that *Oviraptor*, and many other birdlike dinosaurs, had feathers.

BIRD OR DINOSAUR?

As well as finding the first dinosaur nests, the U.S. expeditions to the Gobi Desert in the 1920s uncovered many other dinosaur remains. One of these that we now call *Mononykus* was a total puzzle. Was it a bird or was it a dinosaur? If it was a bird, its arms were too short for it to fly. If it was a dinosaur, what good were hands reduced to a single finger with a big claw? In the 1980s, when new specimens were discovered, *Mononykus* was found to have belonged to a group of related animals, the alvarezsaurids — a distinct group within the maniraptorans — that ranged from South America to Central Asia. Today, we still do not know whether they were birds or dinosaurs.

MONONYKUS

The best known and most complete of the alvarezsaurids was *Mononykus*. It looked like a very lightly built, meat-eating dinosaur with spindly legs and a long tail. The two forelimbs are remarkable. They are short and have a shelf of bone, which in modern birds would support wing feathers, and each bears a single stout, stubby claw. These forelimbs probably evolved from the functional wings of a flying ancestor, such as the Late Jurassic *Archaeopteryx*.

OSTRICH

One function of non-flying wings in modern running birds is for display. The ostrich makes a big show of its wing feathers when it is courting a mate or threatening an enemy. It is quite possible that the part-bird/part-dinosaur animals of the Cretaceous Period also had flamboyant feathers on their flightless wings and used them for display. Unfortunately, such behavior cannot be proven by fossil evidence.

RHEA

A modern rhea, the running bird of today's Argentinian plains, uses its stumpy wings to steer itself while running. Modern flightless birds have evolved from flying ancestors, just as the maniraptorans probably did back in the age of dinosaurs.

PATAGONYKUS

ALVAREZSAURUS

MONONYKUS

THREE ALVAREZSAURIDS

The first alvarezsaurid to be described was *Alvarezsaurus* itself, found in Argentina in the 1970s. This specimen had no forelimbs, so it did not look too unusual, but it did have a very birdlike body. In the early 1990s, good specimens of *Mononykus* were found in Mongolia, and scientists realized these were two very similar animals. In 1991, again in Argentina, the discovery of *Patagonykus* confirmed that there were several related animals in the alvarezsaurid group.

A HALFWAY STAGE

All sorts of other animals seem to have been intermediate in the evolution from dinosaurs to birds. The size of an ostrich, *Unenlagia* was far too big to fly, even though its arms were in the form of small wings. Perhaps these wings helped the animal balance and provided direction control as it ran across open plains. Whatever their function, they probably evolved from the working wings of an ancestor that did fly.

TRIASSIC 248-206 MYA	EARLY/MID JURASSIC 206-159 MYA	LATE JURASSIC 159-144 MYA	EARLY CRETACEOUS 144-97 MYA	LATE CRETACEOUS 97-65 MYA

TERRIBLE HAND

An intriguing fossil from Late Cretaceous rocks in Mongolia shows a pair of arms, 8 feet (2.5 m) long, with three-clawed hands. The animal has been given the name *Deinocheirus*, but we know nothing else about it. The bones look as if they are from an ornithomimid, but they are far bigger than those of any known member of this group. For now, the owner of these extraordinary bones remains a mystery.

GALLIMIMUS SKELETON

Gallimimus, probably the best known of the ornithomimids, had a small, toothless beak. This dinosaur was built for speed and could run at up to 50 miles (80 km) per hour, as fast as a race horse. It usually paced around slowly, stalking small mammals or snapping up seeds and insects, but its speed meant that it could escape from most predators. Its long tail acted as a counterbalance to the front of the body, propelling it forward while it sprinted. Its hipbone also pointed forward. This skeleton is on display at the Natural History Museum in London.

STRUTHIOMIMUS

ORNITHOMIMIDS

All ornithomimids looked similar but varied somewhat in size. *Struthiomimus* was about the size of an ostrich. *Pelecanimimus* was one of the earliest. It had a pouch of skin beneath its long jaws, which had hundreds of tiny teeth. This suggests that the teeth of the group became smaller and smaller before disappearing altogether in the later ornithomimids. *Garidumimus*, named after a mythical Hindu bird, had a small crest on its head. The biggest known was *Gallimimus*, the "chicken mimic" at 13–16 feet (4–5 m) long. Some chicken!

| TRIASSIC 248-206 MYA | EARLY/MID JURASSIC 206-159 MYA | LATE JURASSIC 159-144 MYA | EARLY CRETACEOUS 144-97 MYA | LATE CRETACEOUS 97-65 MYA |

BIRD MIMICS

One group of dinosaurs has always been thought to look very much like birds. Ornithomimids ("bird mimics") had plump, compact bodies; big eyes; toothless beaks on small heads that were supported on long, slender necks; and long legs with thick muscles close to the hip. Typical of the group was *Struthiomimus* ("ostrich mimic") from the Late Cretaceous. Although they fall into the category of meat-eating dinosaurs and would have descended from purely carnivorous ancestors, these dinosaurs were probably omnivorous, eating fruit and leaves as well as insects and small vertebrates, such as lizards. Ostriches and other ground birds of today are also omnivores.

BUILT FOR SPEED

As with most meat-eating dinosaurs, the skeleton of an ornithomimid, such as this *Ornithomimus*, is very birdlike. Balanced by its long tail, its head would have been held farther forward than that of an ostrich. However, it had very similar legs, with a very short femur (thighbone) that would have held all the muscles so the lower leg and the toes were worked only by tendons. This gives a very lightweight leg that could move quickly — a good running leg.

GALLIMIMUS

GARIDUMIMUS

PELECANIMIMUS

EMU

A modern emu is a plains-living animal. The keen eyes in the head, held high on top of a long neck, can spot danger from far across open spaces. Its strong running legs can take it out of danger at great speed. Because of the physical similarity, we think the Late Cretaceous ornithomimids had a similar life on the plains of North America and central Asia.

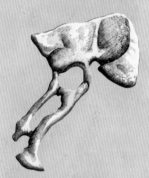

SEGNOSAURUS HIPBONE

The hipbones of meat-eating dinosaurs are usually distinctive. The pubis bone at the front points forward. In the segnosaurids, however, this bone sweeps backward. This is usually only seen in plant-eating dinosaurs, as it gives more space for the big plant-eating intestines that such animals need. Such a pubis bone would have given a segnosaurid's body a very dumpy appearance. This is part of what makes the whole group a puzzle.

SEGNOSAURIDS

Sometimes, part of a skeleton is so unlike any known dinosaur that nobody knows what kind it is. Such is the case with segnosaurids. In the 1920s, the first bones, found in Upper Cretaceous rocks in Mongolia, were thought to be from a giant turtle, but they were reclassified as dinosaur remains in the 1970s. The various bits of bone were so unalike that they seemed to be from different families of dinosaur. Even now, the name therizinosaurid is sometimes used for the group. This name was first used as the original classification of the forelimb, as opposed to segnosaurid, the name chosen when the skull and backbone were studied. These dinosaurs were classified as meat eaters, then as prosauropods, one of the long-necked plant eaters. For the time being, at least, they are back with the meat eaters.

A MODERN PARALLEL

The anteater is a modern animal with claws that seem too big for its body. It uses them to rip through the tough walls of anthills to get at the ant colony. Some scientists have suggested that this is how segnosaurids lived.

TRIASSIC 248-206 MYA	EARLY/MID JURASSIC 206-159 MYA	LATE JURASSIC 159-144 MYA	EARLY CRETACEOUS 144-97 MYA	LATE CRETACEOUS 97-65 MYA

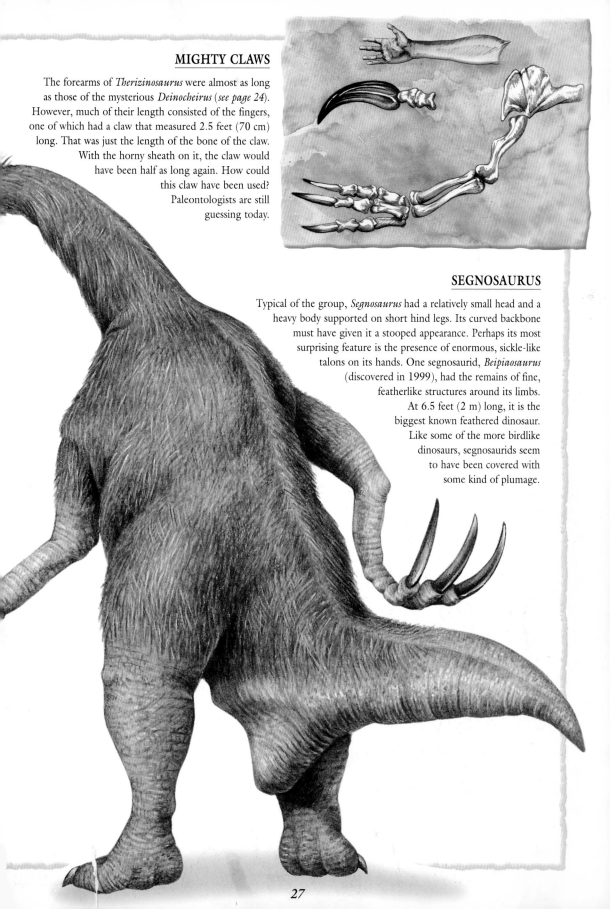

MIGHTY CLAWS

The forearms of *Therizinosaurus* were almost as long as those of the mysterious *Deinocheirus* (*see page 24*). However, much of their length consisted of the fingers, one of which had a claw that measured 2.5 feet (70 cm) long. That was just the length of the bone of the claw. With the horny sheath on it, the claw would have been half as long again. How could this claw have been used? Paleontologists are still guessing today.

SEGNOSAURUS

Typical of the group, *Segnosaurus* had a relatively small head and a heavy body supported on short hind legs. Its curved backbone must have given it a stooped appearance. Perhaps its most surprising feature is the presence of enormous, sickle-like talons on its hands. One segnosaurid, *Beipiaosaurus* (discovered in 1999), had the remains of fine, featherlike structures around its limbs. At 6.5 feet (2 m) long, it is the biggest known feathered dinosaur. Like some of the more birdlike dinosaurs, segnosaurids seem to have been covered with some kind of plumage.

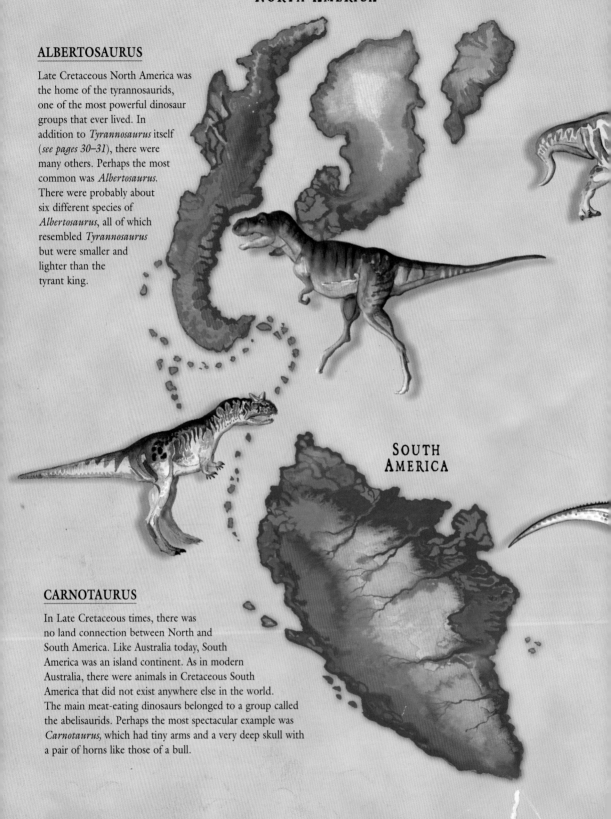

ALBERTOSAURUS

Late Cretaceous North America was the home of the tyrannosaurids, one of the most powerful dinosaur groups that ever lived. In addition to *Tyrannosaurus* itself (*see pages 30–31*), there were many others. Perhaps the most common was *Albertosaurus*. There were probably about six different species of *Albertosaurus*, all of which resembled *Tyrannosaurus* but were smaller and lighter than the tyrant king.

SOUTH AMERICA

CARNOTAURUS

In Late Cretaceous times, there was no land connection between North and South America. Like Australia today, South America was an island continent. As in modern Australia, there were animals in Cretaceous South America that did not exist anywhere else in the world. The main meat-eating dinosaurs belonged to a group called the abelisaurids. Perhaps the most spectacular example was *Carnotaurus,* which had tiny arms and a very deep skull with a pair of horns like those of a bull.

LATE CRETACEOUS ISOLATION

EUROPE

Early in the dinosaur age, all continents of the world were part of Pangaea, a single supercontinent (*see page 9*). It took 150 million years for Pangaea to break up into the continents we know today. At the start of the dinosaur age, the same kinds of dinosaurs lived all over the world. But Earth's surface was splitting apart as rift valleys opened up and formed seas and oceans. Animals then evolved in different ways. By the end of the Mesozoic, meat eaters still lived on each continent but were no longer closely related to those on other landmasses.

ASIA

ASIA'S TYRANNOSAURIDS

The Bering Strait probably did not exist at the start of the age of dinosaurs. North America was joined to Asia by a broad neck of land extending from Alaska, and similar animals lived on both continents. The main big meat eaters in Asia were also tyrannosaurids. *Albertosaurus* did not reach into Asia. Instead, Asia supported tyrannosaurids of its own.

AFRICA

MADAGASCAR

DELTADROMEUS

On the continent of Africa, the biggest of the meat eaters (*see* Carcharodontosaurus, *pages 32–33*) were evolved from animals that resembled *Allosaurus* (*see pages 16–17*). However, there were a number of others, such as *Deltadromeus*, that had evolved from the small meat eaters — the coelurosaurids — of Jurassic times.

MAJUNGASAURUS

The big, meat-eating dinosaur found on the island of Madagascar was *Majungasaurus*. It is interesting that it was an abelisaurid, like the meat eaters of South America and India. This means that before the continents split up, South America, Madagascar, and India were joined together long enough for abelisaurid's ancestors to migrate across all three continents while they were still attached to Antarctica and after Africa had drifted away (abelisaurids are not commonly found in Africa).

TRIASSIC 248-206 MYA	EARLY/MID JURASSIC 206-159 MYA	LATE JURASSIC 159-144 MYA	EARLY CRETACEOUS 144-97 MYA	LATE CRETACEOUS 97-65 MYA

FOOTPRINT

In the late 1980s, a dinosaur footprint almost 3 feet (1 m) long was discovered on a slab of Upper Cretaceous rock in New Mexico. Whatever beast made the print had the claws of a meat eater. There was only one print, so the stride of the animal must have been greater than the almost 10-foot- (3-m-) long slab of rock. Scientists say the animal was moving at 5–6 miles (8–10 km) per hour. We cannot be sure this footprint was made by *Tyrannosaurus*, but we know of no bigger meat-eating dinosaurs in Cretaceous America.

A RANGE OF TYRANNOSAURIDS

Daspletosaurus from North America was similar to *Tyrannosaurus* but was a little smaller and had a heavy head with fewer but larger teeth. At about 20 feet (6 m) long, *Alioramus* was a medium-sized tyrannosaurid from Asia. It had a long skull with knobbles and spikes along the top. The smallest was *Nanotyrannus*, from Montana, at 13 feet (4 m) long. Experts are undecided about this last one. Some think it may have been a small *Albertosaurus*.

TYRANNOSAURIDS

At 39 feet (12 m) long and 20 feet (6 m) tall, *Tyrannosaurus* must have been the scourge of the North American continent at the end of the dinosaur age. So far, about 15 specimens of *Tyrannosaurus* have been discovered in various states of completeness. From these we have a picture of what the mighty beasts looked like. However, there is still much debate about how they lived. Some scientists think they actively hunted, perhaps waiting in ambush for duckbills, the big plant eaters of the time, then charging out at them from the cover of the forest. Others insist they were too big for such activity but would have scavenged carrion, the meat of already-dead animals. Maybe they did both.

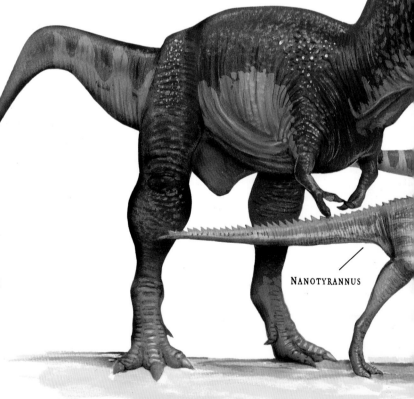

NANOTYRANNUS

FRIGHTFUL BITE

Tyrannosaurus had incredibly powerful jaws and teeth used to rip flesh from its prey. Gouges in the pelvic bone of a Late Cretaceous specimen of the three-horned dinosaur *Triceratops* exactly match the size and spacing of the teeth of *Tyrannosaurus*. From these marks, scientists could tell that a *Tyrannosaurus* bit down into the meat of the hind leg and tore it away from the bone when the *Triceratops* was already dead. But whether it was the *Tyrannosaurus* that killed it, nobody can tell.

TYRANT LIZARD KING

Tyrannosaurus, the biggest of the tyrannosaurids, is often known by its full species name *Tyrannosaurus rex* or simply *T. rex*. Other dinosaurs also have full species names, such as *Allosaurus atrox*, *Velociraptor mongoliensis*, and so on, but these are usually only used by scientists.

DASPLETOSAURUS

ALIORAMUS

COPROLITE

Fossilized animal droppings are known to geologists as coprolites, and they give useful clues to an extinct animal's diet. As with footprints, however, it is often impossible to tell what animal made which coprolite. Big coprolites, more than 8 inches (20 cm) long, that may have come from *Tyrannosaurus*, have been found to contain smashed, undigested bone fragments.

TRIASSIC 248-206 MYA	EARLY/MID JURASSIC 206-159 MYA	LATE JURASSIC 159-144 MYA	EARLY CRETACEOUS 144-97 MYA	LATE CRETACEOUS 97-65 MYA

MONSTROUS SKULL

The skull of *Carcharodontosaurus* is almost completely known. When putting the skull bones together, the scientists only had to recreate the missing front of the snout and the bones at the very rear. This they could do by drawing on their knowledge of other skulls. The final skull is 5 feet (1.5 m) long and has strong, curved, shark-like teeth. We know far less about the skull of *Giganotosaurus*. What we can be sure of is that the jaws were not as powerful as those of *Tyrannosaurus*, the teeth were not as strong, and it had an even smaller brain than the Tyrant Lizard King.

CARCHARODONTOSAURUS

Related to the Jurassic *Allosaurus* (*see pages 16–17*), *Carcharodontosaurus* came from Morocco, in North Africa. Some fossils of this creature were discovered by a German expedition in 1925, but they were destroyed when their museum was bombed during World War II, along with the original remains of *Spinosaurus* found on the same expedition. Only when more fossils were discovered in the mid-1990s did paleontologists realize that *Carcharodontosaurus* was a 50-foot-(15-m-) long giant.

TRIASSIC 248-206 MYA	EARLY/MID JURASSIC 206-159 MYA	LATE JURASSIC 159-144 MYA	EARLY CRETACEOUS 144-97 MYA	LATE CRETACEOUS 97-65 MYA

THE NEW KINGS

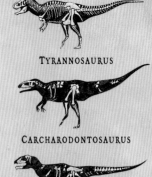

What was the biggest, strongest, and fiercest meat-eating dinosaur that ever lived? *Tyrannosaurus?* Not any more! For the past hundred years we have said that *Tyrannosaurus* was the most powerful of the meat-eating dinosaurs. Generations of scientists have believed this to be so and have even stated that it would be mechanically impossible for bigger meat-eating animals to have existed. But now, the remains of even bigger meat eaters are being found. In the 1990s, the skeletons of two carnivorous dinosaurs were found within a year of one another: one in South America, the other in Africa. Although neither skeleton was complete, they appear to have belonged to a group of dinosaurs that were even longer than *Tyrannosaurus.*

COMPARING KINGS

Both *Carcharodontosaurus* and *Giganotosaurus* were longer than the previous record-holder, *Tyrannosaurus.* As shown above, however, only *Tyrannosaurus* is known from complete skeletons, and there is still a lot we don't know about the other two. Even so, *Tyrannosaurus* seems to have been a much heavier animal and was higher at the hip, so we could still say that the biggest meat-eating dinosaur that is completely known is *Tyrannosaurus.* Still the king!

GIGANOTOSAURUS

The great meat-eating dinosaur *Giganotosaurus* seems to have been closely related to *Carcharodontosaurus,* even though it lived in isolated South America in the Late Cretaceous Period, while the other lived in Africa. It is likely that in the early part of the Cretaceous Period, before the continents were separated by oceans, the ancestors of these animals spread across the whole world. After the continents split apart, *Giganotosaurus* began to evolve separately.

DID YOU KNOW?

• It is very unusual for a dinosaur to form a fossil. Fossils are nearly always of water-living animals. The rocks in which we find fossils are formed of sediment built up on the bottom of seas, lakes, rivers, and sometimes deserts. When a land animal dies, it is eaten by meat-eating scavengers that pull the skeleton to pieces. Any left-over pieces are nibbled away by insects or rotted by bacteria. For a dinosaur to become a fossil, its body would have to fall into water and be immediately buried in sediment where nothing could reach it.

• We only know of about a fifth of the dinosaur species that ever lived. It would be very difficult for a dinosaur living in an upland forest or on a mountain slope ever to become fossilized. Looking at the variety of animals today and their wide range of habitats, scientists estimate that probably between 1,200 and 1,500 different dinosaur species existed. We know of about 300.

• We do not know whether any dinosaur climbed trees. Tree-living animals do not tend to become fossils. The trees are often a long way from the ocean or anywhere that fossils may form. Also, tree-living animals are lightweight, with delicate skeletons that tend to break easily. But some scientists think that maniraptorans developed their curved claws to climb tree trunks and hang on to branches. Some scientists even think that the huge claws of *Deinocheirus* (*see page 24*) were needed by a gigantic sloth-like climbing dinosaur. These ideas are all just scientific theories, however.

• We nearly didn't have the word "dinosaur." In 1832, Herman von Meyer, a German paleontologist, was the first scientist to put these newly discovered animals into their own classification. He called them the "pachypodes." Nine years later, British anatomist Sir Richard Owen set up a classification called "dinosauria," and his word became the accepted one.

MORE BOOKS TO READ

Bigger than T. Rex: The Discovery of the Biggest Meat-Eating Dinosaur Ever Found. Don Lessem (Crown)

Dinosaur Ghosts: The Mystery of Coelophysis. J. Lynett Gillette (Dial Books for Young Readers)

Meat Eaters. Awesome Dinosaurs (series). Michael Benton (Copper Beach)

Tyrannosaurus Rex and Other Cretaceous Meat-Eaters. Daniel Cohen (Capstone)

WEB SITES

Dinosaur Extremes.
  www.enchantedlearning.com/subjects/ dinosaurs/allabout/Extremes.html

The Ferocious Meat-Eaters.
  www.facethemusic.org/fantasy/ dinomeat.html

GLOSSARY

amateur: for enjoyment, not professional.

anatomy: the structure of a body or of an organ. Anatomists study anatomy.

articulated: joined at a certain angle at a joint, often used in explaining how an animal moves.

carrion: dead and decaying flesh.

crest: a decorative part that stands up on the head of a bird or other animal.

drought: a long, dry period of low rainfall.

evolved: changed and developed over long periods of time so that descendants look or behave differently than their early ancestors.

expedition: a journey with a specific goal.

extinct: no longer existing or living.

fossil: a part or impression of an organism from a past geologic age, embedded in natural materials, such as rock or resin.

gullet: the throat or food tube area.

lagoon: a shallow body of water, especially one separated from the sea by sandbars or coral reefs.

mammals: warm-blooded, vertebrate animals, including human beings, that have hair or fur on their skin and nourish their young with milk produced in the mammary glands of the female's body.

migrate: to move to another land area because of a season or climate change.

mimic: to imitate closely, to act or look like.

paleontologist: a scientist who studies fossils to learn about past ages.

Pangaea: the single mass of land that existed on Earth in prehistoric times, before the continents drifted apart.

plumage: the feathers of a bird.

predator: an animal that hunts other animals for food.

prey: an animal that is hunted by another animal for food.

primitive: an earlier, less complex version.

protrude: to push or extend outward.

ranged: could be found in certain areas.

raptor: a bird of prey, such as a hawk.

reptiles: cold-blooded vertebrates, such as snakes, turtles, or crocodiles, that lay eggs and have horny plates or scales.

rift: a deep and narrow cut or opening, usually dividing a rock.

sandstone: rock formed when sediments settle on the bottom of water and harden, joined by cementlike material.

scavenger: an animal that feeds on dead or decaying matter.

sediment: mud and other fine materials that settle at the bottom of water.

serrated: having a toothed, notched cutting edge.

sheath: in animals, a protective tube that surrounds a body part.

sickle: a curved blade used to cut grasses.

snout: the nose or face part that extends forward on an animal.

spawning: when fish lay their eggs.

struts: bars or rods used to hold up or reinforce a structure along its length.

tendon: a band of tough, fibrous tissue that connects a muscle to a bone.

vertebrate: a living organism that has a backbone or spinal column.

INDEX

ACKNOWLEDGEMENTS

The original publisher would like to thank Helen Wire, www.fossilfinds.com, and Elizabeth Wiggans for their assistance.

Picture Credits:
t=top, b=bottom, c=center, l=left, r=right

Lisa Alderson: 4bl, 4/5c, 12/13c, 19t, 22l, 23c, 27c, 33br. John Alston: 4tl, 8/9c, 9t, 14t, 14b, 16tl, 17t, 20cl, 20bl, 23tr, 26tl, 26bl, 27tr, 28/29, 30tl. Corbis: 8tl, 11b, 22b, 23tr, 25tr, 25br, 26cb. Dougal Dixon: 5b, 6b, 10b, 11tl, 11tr, 19b, 33tr. Fossil Finds: 4cl, 14c, 21tr, 31br. Dr Peter Griffith: 15t, 19c. Simon Mendez: Cover (all), 8/9b, 10c, 12-13c, 16/17c, 17b, 18b, 18/19c, 20tl, 24/25c, 31cr, 32c, 34cr. Natural History Museum: 9cr, 12tl, 31t. Oxford City Museum: 6tl, 6c, 6tr. Planet Earth Pictures: 12bl. Luis Rey: 21c, 30/31c. Paul Sereno: 5cr, 32tr.

Every effort has been made to trace the copyright holders, and we apologize in advance for any unintentional errors or omissions.